COLONEL HENRY KING BURGWYN, C.S.A., 1841-1863

Colonel Twentysixth North Carolina Regiment, C.S.A.
Killed at Gettysburg, July 1, 1863, carrying the colors and
leading the charge of his regiment

Dedicated to My Father

COLONEL THOMAS GOODE JONES
General Lee's Flag of Truce bearer at Appomattox
Governor of Alabama 1890-1894.

Confederate War Poems

*Selected and Edited, with an Introduction
and Biographical Data on the Authors*

By

WALTER BURGWYN JONES, LL.B., LL.D.

Publisher
Bill Coats, Ltd.
1406 Grandview Drive
Nashville, Tennessee 37215

First Printing September 1959
Second Printing December 1959
Third Printing July 1961
Fourth Printing March 1974
Fifth Printing March 1984
Sixth Printing March 1987
Seventh Printing March 1990

CONTENTS

FOREWORD

JOHN S. TILLEY, M.A. (Harvard)[1]

Walter Burgwyn Jones is one of the few surviving members of a vanishing race — a race of quiet-spoken, never-blustering Southern patriots on whose escutcheons are blazoned the words "Character, Culture, Courage." One of the "tall fellows ahead of the crowd, a leader of men, marching fearless and proud," his background attests his right to statesman-like qualities. It is a background star-studded with the noblest traditions of the South — a Father with Virginia pride of race in his make-up, a Mother with Tarheel blood in her veins.

It is altogether fitting that this son of a distinguished Confederate Major should be the one to collect and preserve in book form this choice selection of Confederate War Poems. In a career crowded with authorship of legal works, a judgeship of four decades, a presidency of a law school, editorship of a law review, leadership of a Bible Society, he has found time to give expression to his deep-dyed devotion to his Homeland and the Cause which was overwhelmed, but never lost, a Cause which followed a banner bearing the magic words, "States' Rights."

He knows the aptness of the saying, "Let him who will, enact the laws, but let me write the songs of a nation." For the poet who can catch the spirit of a people's emotions and put into words their innermost feelings ranks as one of the leading architects of their future.

In this undertaking is revealed another facet of his many-sided nature. Incarnating, as always, the principle of "Noblesse Oblige," the obligation of one born to the purple to

---

[1]Mr. Tilley, a distinguished Alabama lawyer, practicing at Montgomery, is the author of *Lincoln Takes Command, The Coming of the Glory,* and *Facts the Historians Leave Out.*

share the blessings of life with the less-privileged, he sends this volume forth to mirror the story of days long gone, to inspire the youth of the land with the songs which were sacred to their forebears.

For him it has been a "labor of love," born of devotion to the memory of a past which will ever live in the hearts of the children and grandchildren of the heroes who marched under the "Stars and Bars." He is among those who know that a breed which fails to honor its heroes will soon have no heroes to honor.

THE PRIVATE SOLDIER OF THE CONFEDERACY

The private soldier knows that his valor must pass unnoticed, save in the narrow circle of his company; that his sacrifice can bring no honor to his name, no reputation to his family; that if he survives, it is to enter upon new dangers, with but little hope of distinction; that if he dies he will probably receive only an unmarked grave; and yet he is proud to do his duty and to maintain his part in the destructive conflict. His comrades fall around him thick and fast, but with a sigh and a tear he closes his ranks and presses on to a like destiny. — BISHOP STEPHEN ELLIOTT'S EULOGY, *Southern Literary Messenger*, January, 1863.

PREFACE

The pages which follow contain a collection of Confederate War Poems which, in the years long-gone, "spoke to the heart of the South," and which will endure forever in the minds of our race.

Perhaps the homely definition that poetry is "the best words in the best order" is good enough. But poetry is more than that, for it is, as Ruskin notes, "the suggestion by the imagination of noble grounds for the noble emotions." Macaulay says poetry is the "art of doing with words what the painter does by means of colours." Poetry is one of the fine arts. She is "the queen of the Nine Sisters of the fabled family of the Muses." We of the South take pride in the fact that our Confederate poets wrote songs which make great deeds immortal and composed verses which preserve for us, and for all time, the glorious deeds of captains and chieftains dead and gone.

What a debt of gratitude we owe to our Southern poets! In the days of trial they called our people to virtue, sacrifice, heroism and love. They sang of courage, the power that sustains man in his moments of disappointment and defeat. The soldier of the South heard their song, and hearing, stood steadfast. The poets sang of patience and fortitude. The people of the South heard their music, and hearing, their hearts were made godlike.

In this book the compiler selects a few of what he believes are the greater War Poems of the Confederacy. These poems show the spirit of the stormy times in which they were written and record the patience, the valor and the loyalty of the Confederate soldier.

A reading of these Confederate war poems will awaken memories of renowned warriors and knightly deeds done courageously in defense of home and native land.

Few, if any, of the poems chosen can rank with Henry Timrod's *Magnolia Cemetery Ode;* not all of them attain the height of Randall's *Maryland! My Maryland,* and not all of them are as memorable as Father Ryan's *The Conquered Banner.* Perhaps not all of these I select have poetic merit. Maybe the poet did not always carefully observe the mere mechanical principles of "rime and rythm." Possibly some of the verses have "blind spots." The poems in my thought, however, do all show the spirit of the times in which they were written, and they do preserve the hopes, the triumphs, and sorrows of the Confederacy.

These poems are dear to every Southern heart and they are cherished by our people. They are the household poems recited and loved by a generation now in the grave. They are the verses which embody the traditions and spirit of the Southerner of The Sixties. They are the poems which on thousands of occasions orators recited on Confederate Memorial Days. They are the poems known to every school boy and girl.

The poets who wrote the war poems of the Confederacy were familiar with every form of poetry. They were "skilled masters in word-painting," and when they came to write of their beloved South, her battles, her warriors, and her people, the bards made use of every form known to their art. Our Confederate poets have left us lyrics of surpassing beauty. The ode, the ballad, the elegy, and the monody, each are used to express the poet's feelings and emotions, to tell their stories, and to pay tribute to their valiant countrymen.

The philosophical historian understands that writing history is more than listing some important dates and stating a few bare facts. He knows these do not always explain the meaning of past events and what caused the thoughts and actions of historic personages.

Dr. William Gilmore Simms, in his preface to *War Poetry of the South* aptly observes: "The emotional literature of a people is as necessary to the philosophical historian as the mere details of events in the progress of a nation. This is essential to the reputation of the Southern people, as illustrating their *feelings, sentiments, ideas and opinions* — the motives which influenced their actions, and the objects which they had in contemplation, and which seemed to them to justify the struggle in which they were engaged."

In this same preface, Dr. Simms points out that mere facts seldom indicate the true spirit of the action. He declares that in poetry and song the emotional nature of a people declares itself without reserve and without subterfuge.

Another writer, Charles A. Dinsmore, in *The Great Poets and the Meaning of Life* notes that the poetry and songs of a people present "more directly than history can possibly do the fundamental issues, unencumbered by the incidental and irrelevant. Thus its truth comes with greater clarity and power. The epic poet shows us life as lived by heroes, life magnified by perilous adventure; the lyric poet sings the truth, passionately and musically."

During the years which have passed since Appomattox some critics, especially those of the class which is out to destroy, have contended that many of our most cherished war poems have no poetic rank. These critics, and they never find anything beautiful in the writings of our Confederate poets, are at pains to point out that many of our war poems lack finish, are not the result of mature study, and pay scant attention to the demands of literary art.

We who revere the memory of the Southern Confederacy do not contend that all of her poetry is without "blind spots." This may well be admitted, for the Southern poets depended largely upon inspiration. They did not sit day after day, and hour by hour, and spend weary periods in revising their verse.

Joel Chandler Harris, the beloved "Uncle Remus," once observed: "It is so easy to talk about literary art, and so hard to know what it is. True literary art is the atmosphere of individuality which each mind with a message creates for itself."

The man of common sense knows that a poem reveals its beauty by the effect it has on the emotions and the power it has to lift man nearer to his God and closer to his fellow-man. And so, the war poetry of the Southern Confederacy will live always. Its every stanza is stamped with love of bravery and sacrifice, with admiration for patience and fortitude, and veneration of God.

Nature endowed our poets with great genius. Life in the Confederacy, as it was lived from day to day, presented drama which caused our lyric poets to sing "the truth, passionately and musically."

Nothing relating to the South, her ideals, her soldiers, her battles, her victories and defeats, was foreign to the poets of the Confederacy. From the day the South was first invaded by the hosts of Abolitionists, glorifying the murderer and traitor, Old Brown of Ossawatomie, singing their marching song

> "John Brown's body lies a-mouldering in the grave,
> His soul is marching on!"

until the fateful day when she furled her battle flags after four long years of struggle, the poets of the South wrote daily of her war life. The little every day incidents of camp and march are preserved in stanzas which melt the human heart. The deaths on the field of battle of their leaders produced touching elegies.

The Confederate flag was a constant source of inspiration to our Southern poets. To them it was more than mere cloth. Requier wrote of "the dauntless banner that clove the morning sun" and "streaming swept the night." To Harry McCarthy it was a "Bonnie Blue Flag." Henry Lyndon Flash described it as

> "A beacon that with streaming ray,
> Dazzled a struggling Nation's sight, —
> Seeming a pillar of cloud by day
> Of fire by night."

And to Father Ryan, at the end, it was "The Conquered Banner."

In the centuries to come the memory of the ideals of the Southern Confederacy, her brave soldiers and their heroic deeds, the love and devotion of her women, and the sacrifices of her people, will not be buried beneath the sands of time, and for a great many reasons:

First, because these ideals and traditions deserve to live, and because the contemplation of the lives and deeds of the Southerner of The Sixties and his leaders ennobles and strengthens us.

There is yet, however, another reason why the memory of the Southern Confederacy will live forever — because "poets dead and gone" wrote and sang of the Confederacy in song and verse which will never perish.

Alexander Pope gave utterance to this thought long ago when he wrote.

> "Vain was the chief's, the sage's pride!
> They had no poet, and they died."

The Confederacy had her poets, she lives in history.

A GRAVE IN HOLLYWOOD CEMETERY, RICHMOND[2]

(J. R. T.)

MARGARET JUNKIN PRESTON, 1820-1897

I read the marble-lettered name,
  And half in bitterness I said,
"As Dante from Ravenna came,
  Our poet came from exile-dead."
And yet, had it been asked of him
  Where he would rather lay his head,
This spot he would have chosen. Dim
  The city's hum drifts o'er his grave,
  And green above the hollies wave
Their jagged leaves, as when a boy,
  On blissful summer afternoons,
  He came to sing the birds his runes,
And tell the river of his joy.

Who dreams that in his wanderings wide
  By stern misfortunes tossed and driven,
  His soul's electric strands were riven
From home and country? Let betide
What might, what would, his boast, his pride,
Was in his stricken mother-land,
  That could but bless and bid him go,
Because no crust was in her hand
  To stay her children's need. We know
The mystic cable sank too deep
  For surface storm or stress to strain,
Or from his answering heart to keep
  The spark from flashing back again!

Think of the thousand mellow rhymes,
  The pure idyllic passion-flowers,
Wherewith, in far-gone, happier times,
  He garlanded this South of ours.
Provencal-like, he wandered long,
  And sang at many a stranger's board,
The tenderest pathos through his song.
We owe the Poet praise and tears,
  Whose ringing ballad sends the brave,
Bold Stuart riding down the years.
  What have we given him? Just a grave!

ALL QUIET ALONG THE POTOMAC TONIGHT[3]

THADDEUS OLIVER

"All quiet along the Potomac to-night!"
  Except here and there a stray picket
Is shot, as he walks on his beat, to and fro,
  By a rifleman hid in the thicket.

'Tis nothing! a private or two now and then
  Will not count in the news of a battle;
Not an officer lost! only one of the men
  Moaning out, all alone, the death-rattle.

All quiet along the Potomac to-night!
  Where soldiers lie peacefully dreaming;
And their tents in the rays of the clear autumn moon,
  And the light of their camp-fires are gleaming.

A tremulous sigh, as a gentle night-wind
  Through the forest leaves slowly is creeping;

While the stars up above, with their glittering eyes,
Keep guard o'er the army while sleeping.

There's only the sound of the lone sentry's tread,
As he tramps from the rock to the fountain,
And he thinks of the two on the low trundle bed,
Far away, in the cot on the mountain.

His musket falls slack, his face, dark and grim,
Grows gentle with memories tender,
As he mutters a prayer for the children asleep,
And their mother — "may heaven defend her!"

The moon seems to shine forth as brightly as then —
That night, when the love, yet unspoken,
Leaped up to his lips, and when low-murmured vows
Were pledged to be even unbroken.

Then drawing his sleeve roughly over his eyes,
He dashes off tears that are welling;
And gathers his gun closer up to his breast,
As if to keep down the heart's swelling.

He passes the fountain, the blasted pine-tree,
And his footstep is lagging and weary;
Yet onward he goes, through the broad belt of light,
Towards the shades of the forest so dreary.

Hark! was it the night wind that rustled the leaves?
Was it moonlight so wondrously flashing?
It looked like a rifle: "Ha! Mary, good-bye!"
And his life-blood is ebbing and splashing.

"All quiet along the Potomac to-night!"
No sound save the rush of the river;
While soft falls the dew on the face of the dead,
And the picket's off duty forever!

JOHN R. THOMPSON

ASHBY[4]

JOHN REUBEN THOMPSON, 1823-1873

To the brave all homage render,
   Weep, ye skies of June!
With a radiance pure and tender,
   Shine, oh saddened moon!
"Dead upon the field of glory,"
Hero fit for song and story,
   Lies our bold dragoon.

Well they learned, whose hands have slain him,
   Braver, knightlier foe
Never fought with Moor nor Paynim,
   Rode at Templestowe,
With a mien how high and joyous,
'Gainst the hordes that would destroy us
   Went he forth we know.

Never more, alas! shall sabre
   Gleam around his crest;
Fought his fight; fulfilled his labor;
   Stilled his manly breast.
All unheard sweet Nature's cadence,
Trump of fame and voice of maidens,
   Now he takes his rest.

Earth, that all too soon hath bound him,
   Gently wrap his clay;
Linger lovingly around him,
   Light of dying day;
Softly fall the summer showers;
Birds and bees among the flowers
   Make the gloom seem gay.

There, throughout the coming ages,
    When his sword is rust,
And his deeds in classic pages,
    Mindful of her trust,
Shall Virginia, bending lowly,
Still a ceaseless vigil holy
    Keep above his dust!

THE BONNIE BLUE FLAG[5]

HARRY MCCARTHY

We are a band of brothers
    And native to the soil,
Fighting for the property
    We gained by honest toil;
And when our rights were threatened,
    The cry rose near and far —
"Hurrah for the Bonnie Blue Flag
    That bears the single star!"

CHORUS.

Hurrah! Hurrah!
    For Southern rights hurrah!
Hurrah for the Bonnie Blue Flag
    That bears the single star.

As long as the Union
    Was faithful to her trust,
Like friends and like brothers
    Both kind were we and just;
But now, when Northern treachery
    Attempts our rights to mar,
We hoist high the Bonnie Blue Flag
    That bears the single star. — *Chorus.*

First gallant South Carolina
  Nobly made the stand,
Then came Alabama,
  Who took her by the hand;
Next quickly Mississippi,
  Georgia and Florida
All raised on high the Bonnie Blue Flag,
  That bears the single star. — *Chorus.*

And here's to old Virginia —
  The Old Dominion State —
With the young Confederacy
  At length has linked her fate,
Impelled by her example,
  Now other states prepare
To hoist on high the Bonnie Blue Flag
That bears the single star. — *Chorus.*

Then here's to our Confed'racy,
  Strong are we and brave,
Like patriots of old we'll fight
  Our heritage to save.
And rather than submit to shame,
  To die we would prefer;
So cheer for the Bonnie Blue Flag
  That bears the single star. — *Chorus.*

Then cheer, boys, cheer;
  Raise the joyous shout,
For Arkansas and North Carolina
  Now have both gone out;
And let another rousing cheer
  For Tennessee be given,
The single star of the Bonnie Blue Flag
  Has grown to be eleven. — *Chorus.*

"THE BRIGADE MUST NOT KNOW, SIR"[6]

ANONYMOUS

"Who've we got there?" "Only a dying brother,
   Hurt in the front just now."
"Good boy! he'll do. Somebody tell his mother
   Where he was killed, and how."

"Whom have you there?" "A crippled courier, Major,
   Shot by mistake, we hear.
He was with Stonewall." "Cruel work they've made here;
   Quick with him to the rear!"

"Well, who comes next?" "Doctor, speak low, speak low, sir;
   Don't let the men find out!
It's Stonewall!" "God!" "The brigade must no know, sir,
   While there's a foe about!"

Whom have we here — shrouded in martial manner,
   Crowned with a martyr's charm?
A grand dead hero, in a living banner,
   Born of his heart and arm:
The heart whereon his cause hung — see how clingeth
   That banner to his bier!
The arm wherewith his cause struck — hark! how ringeth
   His trumpet in their rear!

What have we left? His glorious inspiration,
   His prayers in council met;
Living, he laid the first stones of a nation;
   And dead, he builds it yet.

THE BURIAL OF LATANE

THE BURIAL OF LATANE[7]

JOHN REUBEN THOMPSON, 1823-1873

The combat raged not long, but our's the day;
  And through the hosts that compassed us around
Our little band rode proudly on its way,
  Leaving one gallant comrade, glory-crowned,
Unburied on the field he died to gain,
Single of all his men amid the hostile slain.

One moment on the battle's edge he stood,
  Hope's halo like a helmet round his hair,
The next beheld him, dabbled in his blood,
  Prostrate in death, and yet in death how fair!
Even thus he passed through the red gate of strife,
From earthly crowns and palms to an immortal life.

A brother bore his body from the field
  And gave it unto stranger's hands that closed
The calm, blue eyes on earth forever sealed,
  And tenderly the slender limbs composed:
Strangers, yet sisters, who with Mary's love,
Sat by the open tomb and weeping looked above.

A little child strewed roses on his bier,
  Pale roses, not more stainless than his soul.
Nor yet more fragrant than his life sincere
  That blossomed with good actions, brief, but whole:
The aged matron and the faithful slave
Approached with reverent feet the hero's lowly grave.

No man of God might say the burial rite
  Above the "rebel" — thus declared the foe
That blanched before him in the deadly fight,
  But woman's voice, in accents soft and low,
Trembling with pity, touched with pathos, read
Over his hallowed dust the ritual for the dead.

"'Tis sown in weakness, it is raised in power,"
　Softly the promise floated on the air,
And the sweet breathings of the sunset hour
　Came back responsive to the mourner's prayer;
Gently they laid him underneath the sod,
And left him with his fame, his country, and his God.

Let us not weep for him whose deeds endure,
　So young, so brave, so beautiful, he died;
As he had wished to die; the past is sure,
　Whatever yet of sorrow may betide
Those who still linger by the stormy shore,
Change cannot harm him now nor fortune touch him more.

And when Virginia, leaning on her spear,
　Victrix et vidua; the conflict done,
Shall raise her mailed hand to wipe the tear
　That starts as she recalls each martyred son,
No prouder memory her breast shall sway,
Than thine, our early-lost, lamented Latane.

THE CONQUERED BANNER[8]

ABRAM JOSEPH RYAN, 1836-1886

Furl that Banner, for 'tis weary;
Round its staff 'tis drooping dreary;
　Furl it, fold it, it is best;
For there's not a man to wave it,
And there's not a sword to save it,
And there's not one left to lave it
In the blood which heroes gave it;
And its foes now scorn and brave it;
　Furl it, hide it — let it rest!

ABRAM J. RYAN

Take that banner down! 'tis tattered;
Broken is its staff and shattered;
And the valiant hosts are scattered
  Over whom it floated high.
Oh! 'tis hard for us to fold it;
Hard to think there's none to hold it;
Hard that those who once unrolled it
  Now must furl it with a sigh.

Furl that Banner! furl it sadly!
Once ten thousands hailed it gladly,
And ten thousands wildly, madly,
  Swore it should forever wave;
Swore that foeman's sword should never
Hearts like theirs entwined dissever,
Till that flag should float forever
  O'er their freedom or their grave!

Furl it! for the hands that grasped it,
And the hearts that fondly clasped it,
  Cold and dead are lying low;
And that Banner — it is trailing!
While around it sounds the wailing
  Of its people in their woe.

For, though conquered, they adore it!
Love the cold, dead hands that bore it!
Weep for those who fell before it!
Pardon those who trailed and tore it!
  But, oh! wildly they deplored it!
  Now who furl and fold it so.

Furl that Banner! True, 'tis gory,
Yet 'tis wreathed around with glory,
And 'twill live in song and story,
  Though its folds are in the dust:
For its fame on brightest pages,
Penned by poets and by sages,

Shall go sounding down the ages —
   Furl its folds though now we must.

Furl that Banner, softly, slowly!
Treat it gently — it is holy —
   For it droops above the dead.
Touch it not — unfold it never,
Let it droop there, furled forever,
   For its people's hopes are dead!

A REPLY TO THE CONQUERED BANNER[9]

By Sir Henry Houghton, Bart., England

Gallant nation, foiled by numbers!
   Say not that your hopes are fled;
Keep that glorious flag which slumbers,
   One day to avenge your dead.
Keep it, widowed, sonless mothers!
Keep it, sisters, mourning brothers!
Furl it now but keep it still —
   Think not that its work is done.
Keep it till your children take it,
Once again to hall and make it,
All their sires have bled and fought for;
All their noble hearts have sought for —
   Bled and fought for all alone.
All alone! ay, shame the story!
   Millions here deplore the stain;
Shame, alas! for England's glory,
   Freedom called, and called in vain!
Furl that banner sadly, slowly,
Treat it gently, for 'tis holy;
Till that day — yes, furl it sadly;
Then once more unfurl it gladly —
   Conquered banner! keep it still!

DIXIE[10]

Daniel Decatur Emmett, 1815-1904

I wish I was in de land ob cotton,
Old times dar am not forgotten;
   Look away! Look away! Look away! Dixie Land!
In Dixie Land whar I was born in,
Early on one frosty mornin',
   Look away! Look away! Look away! Dixie Land!

Chorus:

Den I wish I was in Dixie! Hooray! Hooray!
In Dixie's Land we'll take our stand, to lib an' die in Dixie.
Away! Away! Away down South in Dixie.
Away! Away! Away down South in Dixie.

Ole missus marry "Will-de-weaber";
Willum was a gay deceaber;
   Look away! Look away! Look away! Dixie Land!
But when he put his arm around her,
He smiled as fierce as a forty-pounder;
   Look away! Look away! Look away! Dixie Land!

His face was sharp as a butcher's cleaber;
But dat did not seem to greab her;
   Look away! Look away! Look away! Dixie Land!
Ole missus acted de foolish part,
And died for a man dat broke her heart;
   Look away! Look away! Look away! Dixie Land!

Now here's a health to de next ole missus,
An' all the gals dat want to kiss us;
   Look away! Look away! Look away! Dixie Land!
But if you want to drive 'way sorrow,
Come hear dis song tomorrow;
   Look away! Look away! Look away! Dixie Land!

DANIEL D. EMMETT

Dar's buckwheat cakes and Injin batter,
Makes you fat or a little fatter;
  Look away! Look away! Look away! Dixie Land!
Den hoe it down an' scratch your grabble,
To Dixie's land I'm bound to trabble;
  Look away! Look away! Look away! Dixie Land!

DREAMING IN THE TRENCHES[11]

WILLIAM GORDON McCABE, 1841-1920

I picture her there in the quaint old room,
  Where the fading fire-light starts and falls,
Alone in the twilight's tender gloom
  With the shadows that dance on the dim-lit walls.

Alone, while those faces look silently down
  From their antique frames in a grim repose —
Slight scholarly Ralph in his Oxford gown,
  And stanch Sir Alan, who died for Montrose.

There are gallants gay in crimson and gold,
  There are smiling beauties with powdered hair,
But she sits there, fairer a thousand-fold,
  Leaning dreamily back in her low arm-chair.

And the roseate shadows of fading light
  Softly clear, steal over the sweet young face,
Where a woman's tenderness blends to-night
  With the guileless pride of a knightly race.

Her hands lie clasped in a listless way
  On the old *Romance* — which she holds on her knee —
Of *Tristram*, the bravest of knights in the fray,
  And *Iseult*, who waits by the sounding sea.

And her proud, dark eyes wear a softened look,
    As she watches the dying embers fall:
Perhaps she dreams of the knight in the book,
    Perhaps of the pictures that smile on the wall.

What fancies, I wonder are thronging her brain,
    For her cheeks flush warm with a crimson glow!
Perhaps — ah! me, how foolish and vain!
    But I'd give my life to believe it so.

Well, whether I ever march home again
    To offer my love and a stainless name,
Or whether I die at the head of my men,
    I'll be true to the end all the same.

ENLISTED TODAY[12]

ANONYMOUS

I know the sun shines, and the lilacs are blowing,
    And summer sends kisses by beautiful May —
Oh! to see all the treasures the spring is bestowing,
    And think my boy Willie enlisted today,

It seems but a day since at twilight, low humming,
    I rocked him to sleep with his cheek upon mine,
While Robby, the four-year old, watched for the coming
Of father, adown the street's indistinct line.

It is many a year since my Harry departed,
    To come back no more in the twilight or dawn:
And Robby grew weary of watching, and started
    Alone on the journey his father had gone.

It is many a year — and this afternoon sitting
    At Robby's old window, I heard the band play,
And suddenly ceased dreaming over my knitting,
    To recollect Willie is twenty today.

And that, standing beside him this soft May-day morning,
    And the sun making gold of his wreathed cigar smoke,
I saw in his sweet eyes and lips a faint warning,
    And choked down the tears when he eagerly spoke:

"Dear mother, you know how these Northmen are crowing,
    They would trample the rights of the South in the dust,
The boys are all fire; and they wish I were going —"
    He stopped, but his eyes said, "Oh, say if I must!"

I smiled on the boy, though my heart it seemed breaking,
    My eyes filled with tears, so I turned them away,
And answered him, "Willie, 'tis well you are waking —
    Go, act as your father would bid you, today!"

I sit in the window, and see the flags flying,
    And drearily list to the roll of the drum,
And smother the pain in my heart that is lying
    And bid all the fears in my bosom be dumb.

I shall sit in the window when summer is lying
    Out over the fields, and the honey-bee's hum
Lulls the rose at the porch from her tremulous sighing,
    And watch for the face of my darling to come.

And if he should fall — his young life he has given
    For freedom's sweet sake; and for me, I will pray
Once more with my Harry and Robby in Heaven
    To meet the dear boy that enlisted today.

THE HOMESPUN DRESS[13]

CARRIE BELLE SINCLAIR.

Oh, yes, I am a Southern girl,
    And glory in the name,
And boast it with far greater pride
    Than glittering wealth or fame.

We envy not the Northern girl,
  Her robes of beauty rare,
Though diamonds grace her snowy neck,
  And pearls bedeck her hair.

Chorus — Hurrah! Hurrah!
  For the sunny South so dear;
Three cheers for the homespun dress
  The Southern ladies wear!

The homespun dress is plain, I know,
  My hat's palmetto, too;
But then it shows what Southern girls
  For Southern rights will do.
We send the bravest of our land,
  To battle with the foe
And we will lend a helping hand —
  We love the South, you know.

Chorus.

Now Northern goods are out of date;
  And since old Abe's blockade,
We Southern girls can be content
  With goods that's Southern made.
We send our sweethearts to the war;
  But, dear girls, never mind —
Your soldier-love will ne'er forget
  The girl he left behind.

Chorus.

The soldier is the lad for me —
  A brave heart I adore;
And when the sunny South is free,
  And when fighting is no more,
I'll choose me then a lover brave
  From all that gallant band;
The soldier lad I love the best
  Shall have my heart and hand.

Chorus.

The Southern land's a glorious land,
  And has a glorious cause;
Then cheer, three cheers for Southern rights,
  And for the Southern boys!
We scorn to wear a bit of silk,
  A bit of Northern lace,
But make our homespun dresses up,
  And wear them with a grace.

Chorus.

And now, young man, a word to you:
  If you would win the fair,
Go to the field where Honor calls,
  And win your lady there.
Remember that our brightest smiles
  Are for the true and brave,
And that our tears are all for those
  Who fill a soldier's grave.

Chorus.

I'M A GOOD OLD REBEL[14]

Innes Randolph, 1837-1887

O, I'm a good old rebel,
  Now that's just what I am;
For this "fair land of freedom"
  I do not care a damn;
I'm glad I fit against it,
  I only wish we'd won,
And I don't want no pardon
  For anything I done.

I hates the Constitution,
  This great Republic too;
I hates the Freedman's Buro,
  In uniforms of blue;

I hates the nasty eagle,
  With all his brags and fuss;
The lyin', thievin' Yankees,
  I hates' em wuss and wuss.

I hates the Yankee nation
  And everything they do,
I hates the Declaration
  Of Independence too;
I hate the glorious Union —
  'Tis dripping with our blood;
I hates their striped banner,
  I fit it all I could.

I can't take up my musket
  And fight 'em now no more,
But I ain't a-going to love e'm,
  Now that is sartin' sure;
And I don't want no pardon
  For what I was and am;
I won't be reconstructed,
  And I don't give a damn.

Three hundred thousand Yankees
  Is stiff in Southern dust;
We got three hundred thousand
  Before they conquered us;
They died of Southern fever,
  And Southern steel and shot;
I wish they was three million,
  Instead of what we got.

I followed old Mas' Robert
  For four year near about,
Got wounded in three places,
  And starved at Point Lookout;
I cotched the roomatism,
  A-camping in the snow,
But I killed a chance o' Yankees —
  I'd like to kill some mo'.

IN THE LAND WHERE WE WERE DREAMING[15]

DANIEL BEDINGER LUCAS, 1836-1909

Fair were our nation's visions, and as grand
As ever floated out of fancy-land;
  Children were we in simple faith,
  But god-like children, whom nor death,
Nor threat of danger drove from honor's path —
  In the land where we were dreaming!

Proud were our men as pride of birth could render,
As violets our women pure and tender;
  And when they spoke, their voices thrill
  At evening hushed the whip-poor-will,
At morn the mocking bird was mute and still,
  In the land where we were dreaming!

And we had graves that covered more of glory,
Than ever taxed the lips of ancient story;
  And in our dream we wove the thread
Of principles for which had bled,
And suffered long our own immortal dead,
  In the land where we were dreaming!

Tho' in our land we had both bond and free,
Both were content, and so God let them be;
  Till Northern glances, slanting down,
  With envy viewed our harvest sun —
But little recked we, for we still slept on,
  In the land where we were dreaming!

Our sleep grew troubled; and our dreams grew wild;
Red meteors flashed across our heaven's field;
  Crimson the Moon; between the Twins
  Barbed arrows flew in circling lanes
Of light, red Comets tossed their fiery manes
  O'er the land where we were dreaming!

DAN'L B. LUCAS

Down from her eagle height smiled Liberty,
And waved her hand in sign of victory;
　　The world approved, and everywhere,
　　Except where growled the Russian bear,
The brave, the good and just gave us their prayer,
　　For the land where we were dreaming!

High o'er our heads a starry flag was seen,
Whose field was blanched, and spotless in its sheen;
　　Chivalry's cross its union bears,
　　And by his scars each vet'ran swears
To bear it on in triumph through the wars,
　　In the land where we were dreaming!

We fondly though a Government was ours —
We challenged place among the world's great powers;
　　We talk'd in sleep of rank, commission,
　　Until so life-like grew the vision,
That he who dared to doubt but met derision,
　　In the land where we were dreaming!

A figure came among us as we slept —
At first he knelt, then slowly rose and wept;
　　Then gathering up a thousand spears,
　　He swept across the field of Mars,
Then bowed farewell, and walked behind the stars,
　　From the land where we were dreaming!

We looked again, another figure still
Gave hope, and nerved each individual will;
　　Erect he stood, as clothed with power;
　　Self-poised, he seemed to rule the hour,
With firm, majestic sway, — of strength a tower,
　　In the land where we were dreaming!

As while great Jove, in bronze, a warder god,
Gazed eastward from the Forum where he stood,
　　Rome felt herself secure and free, —
　　So Richmond, we, on guard for thee,
Beheld a bronzed hero, god-like Lee,
　　In the land where we were dreaming!

As wakes the soldier when the alarum calls, —
As wakes the mother when her infant falls, —
    As starts the traveler when around
    His sleepy couch the fire-bells sound, —
So woke our nation with a single bound —
    In the land where we were dreaming!

Woe! Woe! is us, the startled mothers cried,
While we have slept, our noble sons have died!
    Woe! Woe! is us, how strange and sad,
    That all our glorious visions fled,
Have left us nothing real but our dead,
    In the land where we were dreaming!

And are they really dead, our martyred slain?
No, Dreamers! Morn shall bid them rise again,
    From every plain, — from every height, —
    On which they seemed to die for right,
Their gallant spirits shall renew the fight,
    In the land where we were dreaming!

Unconquered still in soul, tho' now o'er-run,
In peace, in war, the battle's just begun!
    Once this Thyestean banquet o'er,
    Grown strong the few who bide their hour,
Shall rise and hurl its drunken guests from power,
    In the land where we were dreaming!

THE JACKET OF GRAY[16]

Caroline Augusta Ball

Fold it up carefully, lay it aside;
Tenderly touch it, look on it with pride;
For dear to our hearts must it be evermore,
The jacket of gray our loved soldier-boy wore.

Can we ever forget when he joined the brave band
That rose in defense of our dear Southern land,
And in his bright youth hurried on to the fray,
How proudly he donned it — the jacket of gray?

His fond mother blessed him and looked up above,
Commending to Heaven the child of her love;
What anguish was her's mortal tongue cannot say,
When he passed from her sight in the jacket of gray.

But her country had called and she would not repine,
Though costly the sacrifice placed on its shrine;
Her heart's dearest hopes on its altar she lay,
When she sent out her boy in the jacket of gray.

Months passed, and war's thunders rolled over the land,
Unsheathed was the sword, and lighted the brand;
We heard in the distance the sounds of the fray,
And prayed for our boy in the jacket of gray.

Ah vain, all in vain, were our prayers and our tears,
The glad shout of victory rang in our ears;
But our treasured one on the red battle-field lay,
While the life-blood oozed out of the jacket of gray.

His young comrades found him, and tenderly bore
The cold lifeless form to his home by the shore;
Oh, dark were our hearts on that terrible day,
When we saw our dead boy in the jacket of gray.

Ah! spotted and tattered, and stained now with gore,
Was the garment which once he so proudly wore;
We bitterly wept as we took it away,
And replaced with death's white robes the jacket of gray.

We laid him to rest in his cold narrow bed,
And graved on the marble we placed o'er his head
As the proudest tribute our sad hearts could pay —
"He never disgraced it, the jacket of gray."

Then fold it up carefully, lay it aside,
Tenderly touch it, look on it with pride;
For dear must it be to our hearts evermore,
The jacket of gray our loved soldierboy wore!

"JIM—, OF BILOXI"[17]

JAMES LINDSAY GORDON, 1860-1904

"Jim — , of Biloxi." That is all.
It is graven into the granite wall
Where the monument rises fair
Into the soft Virginian air
Among a hundred comrades' names, —
Their country's heritage, — and Fame's.

Jim — , of Biloxi. Nothing more.
Naught of his name or his fame is sure,
Save that down where the river ran
And the regiments struggled man to man,
An humble son of the fighting South
Gave his life at the musket's mouth.

Perchance where the Sunflower River flows
By forests of jessamine and rose,
Or where the Gulf Stream washes far
Its tides of blue to the vesper star,
Some one waited with prayers and tears
For Jim — , of Biloxi, these many years.

Life and Name and Cause all lost;
Least and last of the mightiest host
That ever wrote in the blood of men
A dream that will never be dreamed again,
Gone like the strain that the bugles blew,
Jim — , of Biloxi, heaven shelter you!

JOHN PELHAM[18]

JAMES RYDER RANDALL, 1839-1908

Just as the spring came laughing through the strife
   With all its gorgeous cheer;
In the bright April of historic life
   Fell the great cannoneer.

The wondrous lulling of a hero's breath
   His bleeding country weeps —
Hushed in the alabaster arms of death,
    Our young Marcellus sleeps.

Nobler and grander than the Child of Rome,
    Curbing his chariot steeds;
The knightly scion of a Southern home
    Dazzled the land with deeds.

Gentlest and bravest in the battle brunt,
    The champion of the truth,
He bore his banner to the very front
    Of our immortal youth.

A clang of sabres 'mid Virginian snow,
    The fiery rush of shells —
And there's a wail of immemorial woe
    In Alabama dells.

The pennon drops that led the sabered band
    Along the crimson field!
The meteor blade sinks from the nerveless hand
    Over the spotless shield.

We gazed and gazed upon that beauteous face,
    While 'round the lips and eyes,
Couched in the marble slumber, flashed the grace
    Of a divine surprise.

Oh, Mother of a blessed soul on high!
    Thy tears may soon be shed —
Think of thy boy with princes of the sky,
    Among the Southern dead.

How must he smile on this dull world beneath,
    Fevered with swift renown —
He — with the martyr's amaranthine wreath
    Twining the victor's crown!

                 —March 17, 1863.

LEE TO THE REAR[19]

JOHN REUBEN THOMPSON, 1823-1873

Dawn of a pleasant morning in May,
Broke through the Wilderness cool and gray;
While perched in the tallest tree-tops, the birds
Were carolling Mendelssohn's "Songs without Words."

Far from the haunts of men remote,
The brook brawled on with a liquid note;
And Nature, all tranquil and lovely, wore
The smile of the spring, as in Eden of yore.

Little by little, as daylight increased,
And deepened the roseate flush in the East —
Little by little did morning reveal
Two long glittering lines of steel;

Where two hundred thousand bayonets gleam,
Tipped with the light of the earliest beam,
And the faces are sullen and grim to see
In the hostile armies of Grant and Lee.

All of a sudden, ere rose the sun,
Pealed on the silence the opening gun —
A little white puff of smoke there came,
And anon the valley was wreathed in flame.

Down on the left of the Rebel lines,
Where a breastwork stands in a copse of pines,
Before the Rebels their ranks can form,
The Yankees have carried the place by storm.

Stars and Stripes on the salient wave,
Where many a hero has found a grave,
And the gallant Confederates strive in vain
The ground they have drenched with their blood to regain.

Yet louder the thunder of battle roared
Yet a deadlier fire on the columns poured;
Slaughter infernal rode with Despair,
Furies twain, through the murky air.

Not far off, in the saddle there sat
A gray-bearded man in a black slouched hat;
Not much moved by the fire was he,
Calm and resolute Robert Lee.

Quick and watchful he kept his eye
On the bold Rebel brigades close by,
Reserves that were standing (and dying) at ease,
While the tempest of wrath toppled over the trees.

For still with their loud, deep, bull-dog bay,
The Yankee batteries blazed away,
And with every murderous second that sped
A dozen brave fellows, alas! fell dead.

The grand old gray-beard rode to the space
Where Death and his victims stood face to face,
And silently waved his old slouched hat —
A world of meaning there was in that!

"Follow me! Steady! We'll save the day!"
This was what he seemed to say;
And to the light of his glorious eye
The bold brigades thus made reply:

"We'll go forward, but you must go back" —
And they moved not an inch in the perilous track:
"Go to the rear, and we'll send them to hell!"
And the sound of the battle was lost in their yell.

Turning his bridle, Robert Lee
Rode to the rear. Like waves of the sea,
Bursting the dikes in their overflow,
Madly his veterans dashed on the foe.

And backward in terror that foe was driven,
Their banners rent and their columns riven,
Wherever the tide of battle rolled
Over the Wilderness, wood and wold.

Sunset out of a crimson sky
Streamed o'er a field of ruddier dye,
And the brook ran on with a purple stain,
From the blood of ten thousand foemen slain.

Seasons have passed since that day and year —
Again o'er its pebbles the brook runs clear,
And the field in a richer green is drest
Where the dead of a terrible conflict rest.

Hushed is the roll of the Rebel drum,
The sabres are sheathed, and the cannon are dumb;
And Fate, with his pitiless band, has furled
The flag that once challenged the gaze of the world;

But the fame of the Wilderness fight abides;
And down into history grandly rides,
Calm and unmoved as in battle he sat,
The gray-bearded man in the black slouched hat.

LINES ON A CONFEDERATE NOTE[20]

MAJOR SIDNEY ALROY JONAS,   -1915

Representing nothing on God's earth now,
  And naught in the waters below it,
As the pledge of a nation that's dead and gone,
  Keep it, dear friend, and show it.

Show it to those who will lend an ear
  To the tale that this trifle can tell
Of Liberty born of the patriot's dream,
  Of a storm-cradled nation that fell.

SIDNEY ALROY JONAS

Too poor to possess the precious ores,
 And too much of a stranger to borrow,
We issued to-day our promise to pay,
 And hoped to redeem on the morrow.

The days rolled by and weeks became years,
 But our coffers were empty still;
Coin was so rare that the treasury'd quake
 If a dollar should drop in the till.

But the faith that was in us was strong, indeed,
 And our poverty well we discerned,
And this little check represented the pay
 That our suffering veterans earned.

We knew it had hardly a value in gold,
 Yet as gold each soldier received it;
It gazed in our eyes with a promise to pay,
 And each Southern patriot believed it.

But our boys thought little of price or of pay,
 Or of bills that were overdue;
We knew if it brought us our bread to-day,
 'Twas the best our poor country could do.

Keep it, it tells all our history o'er,
 From the birth of our dream to its last;
Modest, and born of the Angel Hope,
 Like our hope of success, it passed.

LITTLE GIFFEN[21]

Francis Orray Ticknor, 1822-1874

Out of the focal and foremost fire,
Out of the hospital walls as dire,
Smitten of grapeshot and gangrene,
(Eighteenth battle and he sixteen) —

Specter! such as you seldom see,
Little Giffen of Tennessee.

"Take him and welcome," the surgeon said;
Little the doctor can help the dead!
So we took him, and brought him where
The balm was sweet in the summer air;
And we laid him down on a wholesome bed —
Utter Lazarus, heel to head!

And we watched the war with abated breath,
Skeleton boy against skeleton death!
Months of torture, how many such?
Weary weeks of the stick and crutch;
And still a glint in the steel-blue eye
Told of a spirit that wouldn't die.

And didn't. Nay! more! in death's despite
The crippled skeleton learned to write —
"Dear Mother!" at first, of course, and then
"Dear Captain!" inquiring about the men.
Captain's answer: "Of eighty and five,
Giffen and I are left alive."

Word of gloom from the war, one day;
Johnston pressed at the front, they say; —
Little Giffen was up and away!
A tear, his first, as he bade good-by,
Dimmed the glint of his steel-blue eye.
"I'll write, if spared!" There was news of fight,
But none of Giffen — he did not write!

I sometimes fancy that were I King
Of the Princely Knights of the Golden ring,
With the song of the minstrel in mine ear,
And the tender legend that trembles here,
I'd give the best on his bended knee —
The whitest soul of my chivalry —
For "Little Giffen" of Tennessee.

FRANCIS ORRAY TICKNOR

LORENA[22]

Rev. H. D. L. Webster

The years creep slowly by, Lorena,
　The snow is on the grass again;
The sun's low down the sky, Lorena,
　The frost gleams where the flowers have been;
But the heart throbs on as warmly now,
　As when the summer days were nigh;
Oh! the sun can never dip so low,
　Adown affection's cloudless sky.

A hundred months have passed, Lorena,
　Since last I held thy hand in mine;
And felt the pulse beat fast, Lorena —
　Though mine beat faster far than thine;
A hundred months — 'twas flowery May,
　When up the hilly slope we climbed,
To watch the dying of the day,
　And hear the distant church bells chime.

We loved each other then, Lorena,
　More than we ever dared to tell;
And what we might have been, Lorena,
　Had but our lovings prospered well —
But then — 'tis past; the years are gone,
　I'll not call up their shadowy forms;
I'll say to them, "lost years, sleep on!
　Sleep on! Nor heed life's pelting storms."

The story of that past, Lorena,
　Alas! I care not to repeat;
They touched some tender chords, Lorena,
　They lived, but only lived to cheat.
I would not cause e'en one regret
　To rankle in your bosom now —
"For if we try we may forget,"
　Were words of thine long years ago.

Yes, these were words of thine, Lorena —
  They are within my memory yet —
They touched some tender chords, Lorena,
  Which thrill and tremble with regret.
'Twas not the woman's heart which spoke —
  Thy heart was always true to me;
A duty stern and piercing broke
  The tie that linked my soul with thee.

It matters little now, Lorena,
  The past is in the eternal past;
Our hearts will soon lie low, Lorena,
  Life's tide is ebbing out so fast.
There is a future, oh, thank God!
  Of life this is so small a part —
'Tis dust to dust beneath the sod,
  But there, up there, 'tis heart to heart.

THE MAGNOLIA CEMETERY ODE[23]

HENRY TIMROD, 1829-1867

I

Sleep sweetly in your humble graves,
  Sleep, martyrs of a fallen cause;
Though, yet no marble column craves
  The pilgrim here to pause.

II

In seeds of laurel in the earth
  The blossom of your fame is blown,
And somewhere, waiting for its birth,
  The shaft is in the stone!

III

Meanwhile, behalf the tardy years
   Which keep in trust your storied tombs,
Behold! your sisters bring their tears,
   And these memorial blooms.

IV

Small tributes! but your shades will smile
   More proudly on these wreaths today,
Than when some cannon-moulded pile
   Shall overlook this bay.

V

Stoop angels, hither from the skies!
   There is no holier spot of ground
Than where defeated valor lies,
   By mourning beauty crowned!

MY MARYLAND[24]

James Ryder Randall, 1839-1908

The despot's heel is on thy shore,
   Maryland!
His torch is at thy temple door,
   Maryland!
Avenge the patriotic gore
That flecked the streets of Baltimore,
And be the battle queen of yore,
   Maryland! My Maryland!

Hark to an exiled son's appeal,
   Maryland!
My mother State, to thee I kneel,
   Maryland!

For life or death, for woe and weal,
Thy peerless chivalry reveal,
And gird thy beauteous limbs with steel,
   Maryland! My Maryland!

Thou wilt not cower in the dust,
   Maryland!
Thy beaming sword shall never rust,
   Maryland!
Remember Carroll's sacred trust,
Remember Howard's warlike thrust,
And all thy slumberers with the just,
   Maryland! My Maryland!

Come! 'tis the red dawn of the day,
   Maryland!
Come with thy panoplied array,
   Maryland!
With Ringgold's spirit of the fray,
With Watson's blood at Monterey,
With fearless Lowe and dashing May,
   Maryland! My Maryland!

Come! for thy shield is bright and strong,
   Maryland!
Come! for thy dalliance does thee wrong,
   Maryland!
Come to thine own heroic throng,
That stalks with Liberty along,
And ring dauntless slogan-song,
   Maryland! My Maryland!

Dear mother! burst the tyrant's chain,
   Maryland!
Virginia should not call in vain,
   Maryland!
She meets her sisters on the plain —
"*Sic Semper,*" 'tis the proud refrain

That baffles minions back amain,
  Maryland!
Arise in majesty again,
  Maryland! My Maryland!

I see the blush upon thy cheek,
  Maryland!
For thou wast ever bravely meek,
  Maryland!
But lo! there surges forth a shriek
From hill to hill, from creek to creek —
Potomac calls to Chesapeake,
  Maryland! My Maryland!

Thou wilt not yield the Vandal toll,
  Maryland!
Thou wilt not crook to his control,
  Maryland!
Better the fire upon thee roll,
Better the shot, the blade, the bowl,
Than crucifixion of the soul,
  Maryland! My Maryland!

I hear the distant thunder hum,
  Maryland!
The old-time bugle, fife, and drum,
  Maryland!
She is not dead, nor deaf, nor dumb —
Huzzah! she spurns the Northern scum!
She breathes — she burns! she'll come! she'll come!
  Maryland! My Maryland!

MUSIC IN CAMP[25]

JOHN REUBEN THOMPSON 1823-1873

Two armies covered hill and plain,
  Where Rappahannock's waters
Ran deeply crimsoned with the stain
  Of battle's recent slaughters.

The summer clouds lay pitched like tents
  In meads of heavenly azure;
And each dread gun of the elements
  Slept in its hid embrasure.

The breeze so softly blew, it made
  No forest leaf to quiver,
And the smoke of the random cannonade
  Rolled slowly from the river.

And now, where circling hills looked down
  With cannon grimly planted,
O'er listless camp and silent town
  The golden sunset slanted.

When on the fervid air there came
  A strain — now rich, now tender;
The music seemed itself aflame
  With day's departing splendor.

A Federal band, which, eve and morn,
  Played measures brave and nimble,
Had just struck up, with flute and horn
  And lively clash of cymbal.

Down flocked the soldiers to the banks,
  Till, margined by its pebbles,
One wooded shore was blue with "Yanks,"
  And one was gray with "Rebels."

Then all was still, and then the band,
  With movement light and tricksy,
Made stream and forest, hill and strand,
  Reverberate with "Dixie."

The conscious stream with burnished glow
  Went proudly o'er its pebbles,
But thrilled throughout its deepest flow
  With yelling of the Rebels.

Again a pause, and then again
  The trumpets pealed sonorous,
And "Yankee Doodle" was the strain
  To which the shore gave chorus.

The laughing ripple shoreward flew,
  To kiss the shining pebbles;
Loud shrieked the swarming Boys in Blue
  Defiance to the Rebels.

And yet once more the bugle sang
  Above the stormy riot;
No shout upon the evening rang —
  There reigned a holy quiet.

The sad, slow stream its noiseless flood
  Poured o'er the glistening pebbles;
All silent now the Yankees stood,
  And silent stood the Rebels.

No unresponsive soul had heard
  That plaintive note's appealing,
So deeply "Home, Sweet Home" had stirred
  The hidden founts of feeling.

Or Blue, or Gray, the soldier sees
  As by the wand of fairy,
The cottage 'neath the live-oak trees,
  The cabin by the prairie.

Or cold, or warm, his native skies
    Bend in their beauty o'er him;
Seen through the tear-mist in his eyes,
    His loved ones stand before him.

As fades the iris after rain
    In April's tearful weather,
The vision vanished, as the strain
    And daylight died together.

But memory, waked by music's art,
    Expressed in simplest numbers,
Subdued the sternest Yankee's heart,
    Made light the Rebel's slumbers.

And fair the form of music shines,
    That bright celestial creature,
Who still, 'mid war's embattled lines,
    Gave this one touch of Nature.

THE SHADE OF THE TREES[26]

MARGARET JUNKIN PRESTON, 1820-1897

What are the thoughts that are stirring his breast?
    What is the mystical vision he sees?
— "Let us pass over the river, and rest
    Under the shade of the trees."

Has he grown sick of his toils and his tasks?
    Sighs the worn spirit for respite or ease?
Is it a moment's cool halt that he asks
    "Under the shade of the trees."

Is it the gurgle of waters whose flow
    Oftime has come to him, borne on the breeze,
Memory listens to, lapsing so low,
    Under the shade of the trees?

Nay — though the rasp of the flesh was so sore,
    Faith, that had yearnings far keener than these,
Saw the soft sheen of the Thitherward Shore
    Under the shade of the trees; —

Caught the high psalms of ecstatic delight —
    Heard the harps harping, like soundings of seas —
Watched earth's assoiled ones walking in white
    Under the shade of the trees.

Oh, was it strange he should pine for release,
    Touched to the soul with such transports as these, —
He who so needed the balsam of peace,
    Under the shade of the trees?

Yea, it was noblest for him — it was best
    (Questioning naught of our Father's decrees),
There to pass over the river and rest
    Under the shade of the trees!

SOMEBODY'S DARLING[27]

MARIE LaCOSTE,   -1936

Into a ward of the whitewashed halls,
    Where the dead and dying lay,
Wounded by bayonets, shells, and balls,
    Somebody's darling was borne one day —
Somebody's darling, so young and so brave,
    Wearing yet on his pale, sweet face,
Soon to be hid by the dust of the grave,
    The lingering light of his boyhood's grace.

Matted and damp are the curls of gold
    Kissing the snow of his fair, young brow;
Pale are the lips of delicate mold,
    Somebody's darling is dying now.

Back from his beautiful blue-veined brow,
    Brush all the wandering waves of gold,
Cross his hands on his bosom now —
    Somebody's darling is stiff and cold.

Kiss him once for somebody's sake,
    Murmur a prayer soft and low;
One bright curl from its fair mates take —
    They were somebody's pride, you know.
Somebody's hand has rested there:
    Was it mother's soft and white?
Or had the lips of a sister fair
    Been baptized in their waves of light?

God knows best! He has somebody's love,
    Somebody's heart enshrined him there,
Somebody wafted his name above,
    Night and morn, on the wings of prayer.
Somebody wept when he marched away,
    Looking so handsome, brave and grand!
Somebody's kiss on his forehead lay,
    Somebody clung to his parting hand.

Somebody's watching and waiting for him,
    Yearning to hold him again to her heart;
And there he lies with his blue eyes dim,
    And his smiling, child-like lips apart.
Tenderly bury the fair young dead,
    Pausing to drop on his grave a tear;
Carve on the wooden slab at his head,
    "Somebody's darling slumbers here!"

THE SOUTH[28]

ABRAM JOSEPH RYAN, 1839-1894

Yes, give me the land
    Where the ruins are spread,
And the living tread light
    On the heart of the dead;

Yes, give me the land
  That is blest by the dust,
And bright with the deeds,
  Of the down-trodden just.

Yes, give me the land
  Where the battle's red blast
Has flashed on the future
  The form of the past;
Yes, give me the land
  That hath legends and lays
That tell of the memories
  Of long-vanished days.

Yes, give me the land
  That hath story and song
To tell of the strife
  Of the right with the wrong;
Yes, give me the land
  With a grave in each spot
And names in the graves
  That shall not be forgot.

Yes, give me the land
  Of the wreck and the tomb;
There's grandeur in graves —
  There's glory in gloom.
Far out of the gloom
  Future brightness is born;
As, after the night
  Looms the sunrise of morn.

And the graves of the dead,
  With the grass overgrown,
May yet form the footstool
  Of Liberty's throne;
And each simple wreck
  In the way-path of might
Shall yet be a rock
  In the temple of Right.

STONEWALL JACKSON'S WAY[29]

JOHN WILLIAMSON PALMER, 1825-1906

Come, stack arms, men. Pile on the rails,
   Stir up the camp-fire bright;
No matter if the canteen fails,
   We'll make a roaring night.
Here Shenandoah brawls along,
   There burly Blue Ridge echoes strong
To swell the brigade's rousing song
   Of "Stonewall Jackson's way."

We see him now — the old slouched hat
   Cocked o'er his eye askew —
The shrewd, dry smile — the speech so pat —
   So calm, so blunt, so true.
The "Blue-Light Elder" knowns 'em well —
   Says he, "That's Banks; he's fond of shell —
Lord save his soul! we'll give him" well,
   That's "Stonewall Jackson's way."

Silence! ground arms! kneel all! caps off!
   Old Blue Light's going to pray;
Strangle the fool that dares to scoff;
   Attention; it's his way!
Appealing from his native sod,
   In forma pauperis to God —
"Lay bare thine arm; stretch forth thy rod;
   Amen'" That's "Stonewall's way."

He's in the saddle now! Fall in!
   Steady, the whole brigade!
Hill's at the ford, cut off! He'll win
   His way out, ball and blade.
What matter if our shoes are worn?
   What matter if our feet are torn?
"Quick step — we're with him ere the dawn!"
   That's "Stonewall Jackson's way."

The sun's bright glances rout the mists
    Of morning, and, by George!
There's Longstreet struggling in the lists,
    Hemmed in an ugly gorge —
Pope and his Yankees whipped before —
    "Bayonet and grape!" hear Stonewall roar,
"Charge, Stuart! Pay off Ashby's score
    In Stonewall Jackson's way."

Ah, maiden! wait and watch and yearn
    For news of Stonewall's band!
Ah, widow! read with eyes that burn
    That ring upon thy hand!
Ah, wife! sew on, pray on, hope on,
    Thy life shall not be all forlorn —
The foe had better ne'er been born,
    That gets in Stonewall's way.

THE SWORD OF ROBERT LEE[30]

Father Abram Joseph Ryan, 1839-1894

Forth from its scabbard, pure and bright,
    Flashed the sword of Lee!
Far in the front of the deadly fight,
High o'er the brave in the cause of Right
Its stainless sheen, like a beacon light,
    Led us to Victory!

Out of its scabbard, where, full long,
    It slumbered peacefully,
Roused from its rest by the battle's song,
Shielding the feeble, smiting the strong,
Guarding the right, avenging the wrong,
    Gleamed the sword of Lee!

Forth from its scabbard, high in air
   Beneath Virginia's sky —
And they who saw it gleaming there,
And knew who bore it, knelt to swear
That where that sword led they would dare
   To follow — and to die!

Out of its scabbard! Never hand
   Waved sword from stain as free,
Nor purer sword led braver band,
Nor braver bled for a brighter land,
Nor brighter land had a cause so grand,
   Nor cause a chief like Lee!

Forth from its scabbard! How we prayed
   That sword might victor be;
And when our triumph was delayed,
And many a heart grew sore afraid,
We still hoped on while gleamed the blade
   Of noble Robert Lee!

Forth from its scabbard all in vain
   Bright flashed the sword of Lee;
'Tis shrouded now in its sheath again,
Its sleeps the sleep of our noble slain,
Defeated, yet without stain,
   Proudly and peacefully!

"TELL THE BOYS THE WAR IS ENDED"[31]

EMILY J. MOORE

"Tell the boys the war is ended,"
   These were all the words he said;
"Tell the boys the war is ended,"
   In an instant more was dead.

Strangely bright, serene, and cheerful
   Was the smile upon his face,
While the pain, of late so fearful,
Had not left the slightest trace.

"Tell the boys the war is ended,"
   And with heavenly visions bright
Thoughts of comrades loved were blended,
   As his spirit took its flight.
"Tell the boys the war is ended,"
   "Grant, O God, it may be so,"
Was the prayer which then ascended,
   In a whisper deep, though low.

"Tell the boys the war is ended,"
   And his warfare then was o'er,
As, by angel bands attended,
   He departed from earth's shore.
Bursting shells and cannon roaring
   Could not rouse him by their din;
He to better worlds was soaring,
   Far from war, and pain, and sin.

THE VIRGINIANS OF THE VALLEY[32]

Francis Orray Ticknor, 1822-1874

The knightliest of the knightly race
   Who, since the days of old,
Have kept the lamp of chivalry
   Alight in hearts of gold:
The kindliest of the kindly band
   Who, rarely hating ease,
Yet rode with Spotswood round the land,
   And Raleigh round the seas;

Who climbed the blue Virginia hills
   Against embattled foes,
And planted there, in valleys fair,
   The lily and the rose;
Whose fragrance lives in many lands,
   Whose beauty stars the earth,
And lights the hearths of happy homes
   With loveliness and worth.

We thought they slept! the sons who kept
   The names of noble sires,
And slumbered while the darkness crept
   Around their vigil-fires;
But aye the "Golden Horseshoe" Knights
   Their old Dominion keep,
Whose foes have found enchanted ground,
   But not a knight asleep!

WE'RE TENTING TONIGHT[33]

WALTER KITTREDGE

We're tenting tonight on the old camp ground,
   Give us a song to cheer our weary hearts,
A song of home,
   And friends we love so dear.

We've been tenting tonight on the old camp ground
   Thinking of days gone by,
Of the loved ones at home that gave us the hand,
   And the tear that said "good-by"

We are tired of war on the old camp ground,
   Many are dead and gone,
Of the brave and true who've left their homes,
   Others been wounded long.

We've been fighting today on the old camp ground,
   Many are lying near;
Some are dead and some are dying,
   Many are in tears.

Many are the hearts that are weary tonight,
   Wishing for the war to cease;
Many are the hearts looking for the right,
   To see the dawn of peace.

Tenting tonight,
   Tenting tonight,
Tenting on the old camp ground,
   Dying tonight,
Dying on the old camp ground.

YOUR LETTER, LADY, CAME TOO LATE[34]

Colonel William S. Hawkins

Your letter, lady, came too late,
   For Heaven had claimed its own.
Ah, sudden change! from prison bars
   Unto the Great White Throne!
And yet, I think he would have stayed
   To live for his disdain,
Could he have read the careless words
   Which you have sent in vain.

So full of patience did he wait
   Through many a weary hour,
That o'er his simple soldier faith
   Not even death had power.
   And you — did others whisper low
   Their homage in your ear,
As though among their shadowy throng
   His spirit had a peer.

I would that you were by me now,
    To draw the sheet aside,
And see how pure the look he wore
    The moment when he died.

The sorrow that you gave him
    Had left its weary trace,
As 'twere the shadow of the cross
    Upon his pallid face.

"Her love," he said, "could change for me
    The winter's cold to spring."
Ah, trust of fickle maiden's love,
    Thou art a bitter thing!
For when these valleys bright in May
    Once more with blossoms wave,
The northern violets shall blow
    Above his humble grave.

Your dole of scanty words had been
    But one more pang to bear,
For him who kissed unto the last
    Your tress of golden hair.
I did not put it where he said,
    For when the angels come
I would not have them find the sign
    Of falsehood in the tomb.

I've seen your letter and I know
    The wiles that you have wrought
To win that noble heart of his,
    And gained it — cruel thought!
What lavish wealth men sometimes give
    For what is worthless all:
What manly bosoms beat for them
    In folly's falsest thrall.

You shall not pity him, for now
  His sorrow has an end,
Yet would that you could stand with me
  Beside my fallen friend.

And I forgive you for his sake
  As he — if it be given —
May even be pleading grace for you
  Before the court of heaven.

Tonight the cold wind whistles by
  As I, my vigil keep
Within the prison dead house, where
  Few mourners come to weep.
A rude plank coffin holds his form,
  Yet death exalts his face
And I would rather see him thus
  Than clasped in your embrace.

Tonight your home may shine with lights
  And ring with merry song,
And you be smiling as your soul
  Had done no deadly wrong.
Your hand so fair that none would think
  It penned these words of pain;
Your skin so white — would God, your heart
  Were half as free from stain.

I'd rather be my comrade dead,
  Than you in life supreme:
For yours the sinner's waking dread,
  And his the martyr's dream.
Whom serve we in this life we serve
  In that which is to come:
He chose his way, you yours; let God
  Pronounce the fitting doom.

C.S.A.

FATHER ABRAM JOSEPH RYAN, 1838-1886

Do we weep for the heroes who died for us,
Who living were true and tried for us,
And dying sleep side by side for us;
   The Martyr-band
   That hallowed our land
With the blood they shed in a tide for us?

Ah! fearless on many a day for us
They stood in front of the fray for us,
And held the foeman at bay for us;
   And tears should fall
   Fore'er o'er all
Who fell while wearing the Gray for us.

How many a glorious name for us,
How many a story of fame for us
They left: Would it not be a blame for us
   If their memories part
   From our land and heart,
And a wrong to them, and shame for us?

No, no, no, they were brave for us,
And bright were the lives they gave for us;
The land they struggled to save for us
  Will not forget
  Its warriors yet
Who sleep in so many a grave for us.

On many and many a plain for us
Their blood poured down all in vain for us,
Red, rich, and pure, like a rain for us;
  They bleed—we weep,
  We live—they sleep,
"All lost," the only refrain for us.

But their memories e'er shall remain for us,
And their names, bright names, without
      stain for us;
The glory they won shall not wane for us,
  In legend and lay
  Our heroes in Gray
Shall forever live over again for us.

NOTES

[2] Margaret Junkin Preston was born May 19, 1820, at Philadelphia and died in Baltimore, March 29, 1897. Her father, the founder of LaFayette College in Pennsylvania, later became President of Washington College at Lexington, and in 1857, the poet was married to Professor J. L. T. Preston of the Virginia Military Institute. An excellent biography and critical study of her poetry is found in Hubner's *Representative Southern Poets* (1906) at pages 148-165. In Park's *Southern Poets* (1936) at p. 393, is a brief biographical sketch of the poet and on p. 153 appears her poem, "The Shade of the Trees".

[3] This poem was a great favorite among Confederate soldiers and the people of the South. The authorship of the poem is attributed to Lamar Fontaine and sometimes to Mrs. Randolph Harrison. See *Confederate Scrapbook* (Richmond, Va.) 1893, pp. 148-149 where the poem is printed and also an account of how the poem came to be written. In *Southern Life in Southern Literature* (Fulton) p. 262, the poem is printed with a note stating that the poet, Thaddeus Oliver was born in Twiggs County, Georgia, in 1826. He was an eloquent lawyer and a gifted man. He died in a hospital at Charleston, South Carolina, in 1864.

In the *Library of Southern Literature*, Atlanta, 1907, Vol. XV, p. 150 appears a sketch of Lamar Fontaine and he is credited with being the author of *All Quiet Along the Potomac Tonight*, and on p. 326 of the same volume appear a sketch of Thaddeus Oliver with the notation that "there is abundant evidence for his claim to the authorship of the famous war lyric 'All Quiet Along the Potomac Tonight' ". The compiler of this volume, after long and thoughtful study, is convinced that Thaddeus Oliver is the author of the poem.

[4] A biographical and critical sketch of the poet can be found in Vol. XII, p. 5227 of the *Library of Southern Literature*. A brief sketch of the poet is also found at p. 392 of *Southern Poets* (Parks); in Fulton's *Southern Life in Southern Literature* (1907) will be found a sketch of the poet at page 248 and on pp. 250-252 will be found his poem *Music In Camp* and on p. 253 will be found his poem *The Burial of Latane*.

[5] *The Bonnie Blue Flag* was first sung January 9, 1861, in a Jackson, Mississippi, theatre. See *Official and Statistical Register*, 1908, "Capitol Buildings of Mississippi," pp. 197-198. The song was composed by an Irish actor, Harry McCarthy, who enlisted in the Con-

federate Army, from Arkansas. Regrettably we know very little of the life of this Southern singer and actor, and we have no record of any other writings by him. He served in the Confederate Army for awhile, was granted a discharge and became a member of a traveling troupe of actors. He died in Arkansas in 1874.

[6] Stonewall Jackson is justly the subject of more poems than any other Confederate officer. The occasion of his mortal wounding and subsequent death brought forth many touching elegies. An anonymous Confederate poet wrote a touching poem entitled, *The Brigade Must Not Know, Sir!* This poem is based on the incident when Jackson was fired upon and mortally wounded by his own men.

You recall that he rode through the lines at Chancellorsville giving orders to the outposts to fire on any who came along their road. The General did not expect to return that way himself. Later he changed his mind, and as he and several of his staff officers and couriers rode in the dark, Jackson's own men mistook him for the enemy, and, obedient to orders, fired into the group. General Jackson was fatally wounded and as they helped him to the rear he told the officer who was assisting him if any asked who was wounded, "Just say it is a Confederate officer. The brigade must not know, Sir, that I am wounded."

[7] The most classic poem of the War Between the Union and the Confederacy, according to Lord Tennyson, is the *Burial of Latane* by John Reuben Thompson of Virginia. This poem tells the pathetic story of the burial in the peaceful garden of an old Virginia home of a gallant Confederate captain who was killed in hand-to-hand conflict with the foe.

During General "Jeb" Stuart's famous raid around the rear of Major General George B. McClellan's army as it lay before Richmond in 1862, only one man was killed, Capt. William Latane. His younger brother, James, was also in the fight. After the battle was over he met an old farm cart going to a nearby farm. He placed his brother's body on it and took it to nearby *Westwood*, the family seat of Mrs. Catherine Brockenborough and there left it with the good woman for burial.

James Latane, on his sad and lonely errand, was met by a party of federal troops who "followed him to Mrs. Brockenborough's gate, and stopping there, told him that as soon as he had placed his brother's body in friendly hands he must surrender himself a prisoner of war."

Mrs. Brockenborough sent one of her slaves for an Episcopal minister to read the burial service, but the federal pickets would not allow the clergyman to pass through their lines. So, after waiting until sunset on the afternoon of the following day, Mrs. Brockenborough had a servant, "Old Aaron," dig a grave in her garden. Standing at the head of the grave, she read the burial service of the Protestant Episcopal Church in the presence of a few weeping women, two little girls, and some faithful darkies.

8 Abram Joseph Ryan (1838-1886), lovingly known as "Father Ryan," is often called the "poet-priest of the Confederacy." He was born in Norfolk, Virginia, in 1838, of parents who a few years before had emigrated from Ireland.

'Father Ryan' was educated for the priesthood of the Roman Catholic Church and was ordained as a priest a short time before the guns roared at Sumter. He served throughout the war as a chaplain in the Confederate Army. After the war he lived in various parts of the South. In Augusta, Georgia, 'Father Ryan' founded a weekly magazine known as the *Banner of the South* and wrote most of his war poems for this magazine. He lived for a time after the war near "Beauvoir" and became an intimate friend of President Davis and his family.

The poem by which we best remember Father Ryan is *The Conquered Banner,* first printed under the pen-name, "Moina."

Father Ryan has been one of the most widely-read poets in America. To read his poems is to love poetry. He was a Southerner of the most pronounced kind and was unwilling to make any concession to the victorious opponents of the South. As we study the poems of this noble poet and priest, we note that the most characteristic trait of Father Ryan's verse is its unaffected sadness. We note also the simple sublimity of his verse, the beauty of his conceptions, the grandeur of his thoughts, and the refined elegance of the phrases he used.

Father Ryan's poems will live through the ages. They bear the stamp of genius, are impressed with the majesty of truth, and are replete with the power of love. *The Conquered Banner* is often referred to as "the requiem of the Lost Cause."

This beautiful poem was written one afternoon soon after General Lee's surrender. The poet's mind was engrossed with thoughts of the Southern soldier dead and of the cause for which they gave their lives. The composition of the poem took less than an hour. In it Father Ryan not only expressed his own deep emotions, but echoed the unuttered feelings of the Southern people.

9 Baron Houghton (1809-1885) was an English poet and man of letters. He was the author of several volumes of graceful verse and was a patron of young writers. See Webster's *Biographical Dictionary.* (First Ed., 1943; *II Encyclopedia Brittanica,* 801, 1952 Ed.).

10 The Northern writer who was given the study in the *Cambridge History of American Literature* of 'Patriotic Songs and Hymns' makes

the distinction: "They stand in deference to the tradition of 'The Star Spangled Banner,' but they rise to 'Dixie' itself."

The author of the song, *Dixie*, "the national air of the Southern Confederacy," is Daniel Decatur Emmett (1815-1904), a Northerner by birth, but a Southerner in all his sentiments. He served as a fifer in the United States army for awhile, later became a minstrel trouper, and wrote many popular songs; but we remember him today because he wrote *Dixie*.

One rainy Sunday in New York City, September, 1859, he wrote *Dixie*. The words of the song were hastily written and were later modified by the author. *Dixie* was sung in New Orleans during the winter of 1860-61. Immediately the South adopted the song as its own.

The words of Emmett's *Dixie* were written for a minstrel show, and not for a national anthem, so efforts have been made to get a literary *Dixie*. Gen. Albert Pike's version is perhaps the best, though somewhat pompous. But *it is the melody of the song*, not its words, *which endears Dixie to the people of the South*.

We have no martial song in our country which so stirs the emotions as *Dixie* does. Theodore Roosevelt declared: *"Dixie is our only piece of martial music. It is the best battle music in the world."*

[11] The poets of the South wrote of many, many things; but ever their thoughts turned homeward, and much of the exquisite poetry of the War deals with scenes at home. William Gordon McCabe (1841-1920) who was the son of an Episcopal minister and poet, entered the University of Virginia in 1861. Immediately upon the Secession of his State, he entered the Confederate Army and served with distinction and gallantry all through the war. After the war he won fame as a teacher of young men. His poem *Dreaming in the Trenches* is one of the sweetest poems to come out of the War for Southern Independence.

[12] This poem found in *Southern Poems of the War*, Miss Emily V. Mason (1868), contains the following note: The lines of this poem "were found on the body of a young soldier belonging to one of the Alabama regiments in General Lee's army, and are supposed to have been written by his mother, as none but a mother's loving heart could have prompted such exquisite sentiments." The poem also can be found at p. 225 of *War Songs and Poems of the Southern Confederacy*, (1904) collected by Dr. H. M. Wharton.

[13] Carrie Belle Sinclair, the author of this poem, was born in Georgia in 1839. She was a niece of Robert Fulton, inventor of the steamboat. During the War, she devoted much time to caring for the wounded soldiers in the Confederate hospitals at Savannah. She wrote many poems besides *The Homespun Dress*. A collection of her poems appeared in 1872 entitled *Heart Whispers or Echoes of Spring*.

14 This poem is found on p. 144 of *Southern Poets* (Parks) 1936 and there on p. 391 will be found a sketch of the poet. He was born in Winchester, Virginia in 1837 and died in 1887. After serving in the Confederate Army, he became a lawyer and practiced at Baltimore. For many years before his death, he was an editorial writer for the Baltimore *American*.

15 Daniel Bedinger Lucas, 1836-1909, was born near Charles Town, Virginia, now West Virginia. He graduated from the University of Virginia in 1854, studied law at Lexington, and was graduated with high honors in 1859. In 1889, he became a member of the Virginia State Supreme Court of Appeals. His verse was collected by his daughter, Virginia, in 1913. *In the Land Where We Were Dreaming* was first published in the Montreal (Canada) *Gazette*. It was composed a short time after the surrender of General Lee, and while the author was in Canada on a mission to aid a friend held on a charge of treason.

16 *The Jacket of Gray* was written by Mrs. Ball in Charleston, South Carolina and was first published in 1866. After the War for Southern Independence, Mrs. Ball wrote many other poems of great merit. She was born in 1825.

17 In the Days of The Sixties, a mere stripling from Biloxi heard the call of his Southland, under attack and invasion, and without an hour's delay put aside his blue back speller, and his McGuffey's reader, left the sports of his boyhood, his home and friends, and took a private's place in the long columns of Lee and Jackson as they fought for the Constitution on old Virginia's battlefields.

This lad fought with reckless daring in many a great battle and then one summer day fell in the front line, breast to the enemy.

This young Mississippian had been reassigned to the regiment in which he was serving just a few days before the engagement in which he was killed, and was known to his comrades by the name, "Jim——— of Biloxi." His ashes rest peacefully today in that section of the University of Virginia Cemetery at Charlottesville set apart for the Confederate Dead, where stands a monument to the memory of the Confederate soldiers sleeping there. On the monument are chiseled the names and the States from which these soldiers came.

It was impossible to obtain the identity of the young soldier from Mississippi, so they carved on the monument this simple record: "Jim ——— of Biloxi."

One day, many years later, James Lindsay Gordon, a talented poet of the Old Dominion, standing with bared head in the little cemetery, read the inscription, was touched and wrote the unforgettable lines of "*Jim —, of Biloxi*."

[18] James Ryder Randall, author of *Maryland, My Maryland*, like Cooke, was also touched by the heroic death of Pelham. Randall was on military duty at Selma, Alabama, when the body of Pelham arrived there on the way for burial at his old home. In the railroad station there the poet gazed upon "Pelham's face through the glass cover of the coffin" and almost immediately wrote his beautiful stanzas, *Pelham*, in memory of the great cannoneer.

[19] See note 4 ante.

[20] Major S. A. Jonas, of Aberdeen, Mississippi, for many years editor of the *Aberdeen Examiner* and during the war one of General Stephen D. Lee's staff officers, is the author of the poem *Lines on a Confederate Note*.

After General Johnson's surrender, Major Jonas went to High Point, N.C., to secure transportation home. He stopped at the Powhatan Hotel with some fellow officers. While there they met a young lady from the North, a member of a theatrical troupe. She showed them some $500 Confederate notes printed only on one side, which she was taking home as souvenirs. She handed one of the notes to each of the Confederate officers to whom she was talking and asked each to write something "as an autograph" for her on the back of the bills. The officers complied with her request, and what is now known as *Lines on a Confederate Note* is what Major Jonas wrote for the young lady. He had written the verses sometime before and "simply copied them upon the note."

The poem of five stanzas has dignity and restraint. It accepts the outcome of the war calmly and without bitterness, but with pride for gallant deeds and sorrow for the dead.

[21] One of the touching ballads that comes to us from the Days of the Sixties and one which teaches heroic qualities, is *Little Giffen*, written by Dr. Francis Orray Ticknor (1822-1874), telling a story true from beginning to end, and one which illustrates the loyalty of the poorer classes of the South to the cause of the Southern Confederacy.

A boy-soldier yet in his early teens, Isaac Newton Giffen, the son of an East Tennessee blacksmith, was frightfully wounded at Murfreesboro. He was removed to an improvised war hospital in Georgia. The ladies of Columbus visited the hospital wards daily, doing all in their power to alleviate the suffering of the wounded.

One September day, in 1863, Mrs. Ticknor, the wife of a kindly country doctor living at *Torch Hill*, near Columbus, passed through the wards on her daily errands of mercy. She saw the soldier, hardly more than a boy, lying on a cot, emaciated, pale and suffering. She raised his head to give him some needed medicine, and the great mother-heart of this noble woman went out to the lonely boy so far from home. At her request Dr. Ticknor was permitted to take the wounded lad to their home where he could be given better attention.

Little Giffen remained with the Ticknors from September, 1863, to March, 1864. For seven months Mrs. Ticknor tenderly nursed the boy-soldier. She taught him to read and write. The gentle Doctor gave him the best professional skill, and the boy was literally nursed back to life. Then one day news came that General Joseph E. Johnston, the boy's old commander, was being sorely pressed by the enemy, perhaps in the battles of Dallas and Kennesaw Mountain. Quickly Little Giffen left the kindly country doctor and his good wife to go back into battle. A short time later he died for the South in one of the battles around Atlanta.

It is this incident, so touching and so inspiring, which Dr. Ticknor preserves in a ballad which tells one of the noblest stories in all history. Paul Hamilton Hayne declares that *Little Giffen* "is a ballad of such unique and really transcendent merit that . . . it ought to rank with the rarest gems of modern poetry."

22 Boys fight most of our wars, and when boys go from their homes to war they must leave their sweethearts behind. While the boy-soldier of the South was at the front he never forgot the girl he left at home. He sang of her in the camp and she sang of him in the home, both with the hope that they would soon meet again.

One of the most tuneful of all the Confederate songs is *Lorena* which attained wide popularity among the soldiers. It was sung nightly around the camp fires of the Confederacy. The words of this beloved song were written in 1856 by the Rev. H. D. L. Webster, a Presbyterian minister. He wrote the song when twenty-four years old and at a time when he was pastor of a church at Lanesville, Ohio.

A young girl of nineteen, Ella Blockston, sang in the church choir. She and the minister fell deeply in love, but there was family opposition, then a separation, bitter tears and a tragic farewell. Some years later the lover wrote the poem. He met a composer who asked him for words to go with a new piece of music the composer had just written. At that time the poem was called *Bertha*. The poem was accepted, but in order to go with the music a name with three syllables was needed, and so the name *Lorena* was used.

23 In 1867, when the people of Charleston decorated the graves of the Confederate soldiers buried in Magnolia Cemetery, Henry Timrod (1829-1867) wrote the ode sung on that historic occasion. It is known as the *Ode for Decoration Day in Magnolia Cemetery*. It is generally agreed that this Ode is "the most beautiful thing of its kind in conception, tone, and technique, in our national literature." Professor Trent

says the Ode "approximates perfection." This and his other poems establish Timrod "among the genuine lyrical poets of America."

Timrod was an intense Southerner; he loved the South and he loved his native State, South Carolina. Of her he wrote in one of his letters: "No fairer land hath fired a poet's lays, or given a home to man."

Many consider Timrod "the most masterly Southern poet our civilization has produced." This estimate is, perhaps, too high, but certainly Timrod ranks along with Poe and Lanier, and as a writer of Southern war poems Timrod takes first rank. Paul Hamilton Hayne, a poet of great ability himself, declared that Timrod is "one of the truest and sweetest singers this country has given to the world." Tennyson said that Timrod deserved to be called the "laureate of the South."

24 On April 19, 1861, four days after Lincoln's call for 75,000 volunteers to invade the South and attack a people who asked only that the Constitution of the United States be respected, the Sixth Massachusetts Regiment, responding to the call of Lincoln passed through Baltimore on its way to Washington. The Governor of Massachusetts for months before, preparing for an attack on the South, had trained and equipped five thousand soldiers.

A conflict took place between the Massachusetts soldiers and the citizens of Baltimore. Four soldiers were killed. The Federal troops fired upon citizens congregated at a place far away from the point at which the conflict took place and killed several of them. Baltimore was in a frenzy.

At this time James Ryder Randall, of Maryland, intensely southern in sympathy was teaching at Poydras College, Point Coupee, La. One of the citizens killed in the Baltimore conflict was a friend and college mate of Randall. Randall was so stirred by the invasion of his native State and the killing of his friend that when he heard the news he could not sleep. One night (April 23) he left his bed, took his place at an old desk in a second-story room of Poydras College and wrote the most famous and stirring of all Confederate war poems.

It has always been known that the meter of *My Maryland!* was taken from *Karamanian Exile,* by James Clarence Magnan, a gifted Irish poet. One stanza reads:

"I see thee ever in my dreams,
  Karaman!
Thy hundred hills, thy thousand streams,
  Karaman, O Karaman!
As when thy gold-bright morning gleams,
As when the deepening sunset seams

With lines of light thy hills and streams
    Karaman!
So now thou loomest on my dreams,
    Karaman, O Karaman!"

Randall read his poem to one of his classes the morning after writing the poem. In a day or two the poem was printed in the New Orleans *Delta.*

The poem was soon set to music, the best adaptation being to the stately measure of *Tannebaum, O Tannebaum.*

This song breathes the spirit of true patriotism. In the author we have another incident of a poet made famous by one song.

[25] One of the most affecting poems of the War between the Union and the States tells a true incident of the Battle of Fredericksburg. This poem by John R. Thompson (1823-1873) is found in nearly every collection of Southern war poems.

In *Music in Camp* the poet describes the Federal and Confederate armies which were encamped on opposite banks of the Rappahannock and the effect which was had on the soldiers of the Blue and the Gray when the bands of both armies played "Home, Sweet Home."

[26] See note 2 ante.

[27] A poem greatly loved by all Confederates, *Somebody's Darling*, was written by Marie La Coste. She was a Savannah woman and was born in Georgia of French parents and here she devoted her life to teaching French. Miss La Coste wrote one other poem, *In Memoriam.* These verses were dedicated to Captain Joseph Clay Habersham, who was killed in action and to whom Miss La Coste was betrothed. See *Savannah Morning News* (Sav., Georgia), Thursday, July 28, 1938, p. 16, col. 6.

The poem *Somebody's Darling* touched the heart of the South as few poems have. Miss La Coste visited the wounded soldiers brought to Savannah, conforted them with fruits and flowers. The poem was written when the heroic soldiers of the Confederacy were dying daily in the hospital wards at Savannah. The sight of a young soldier, name and regiment unknown, who was fatally wounded, inspired the poem, *Somebody's Darling.*

[28] See note 8 ante.

[29] This was one of the most popular of all the Confederate War Poems, and appears in practically every collection of Southern War Poems:

See *Southern Poets*, Parks, 151, for the poem, and p. 392 for biographical sketch. See *Rebel Rhymes*, Moore, p. 185. See *A Study in Southern Poetry*, Stockard, p. 123; biographical sketch; 125 poem.

See *The South in History and Literature,* Rutherford, 267, biographical sketch and poem p. 268. See *Southern Poems of the War,* Mason, p. 325. See *War Lyrics and Songs of the South,* p. 23. See *Confederate Scrapbook,* 220. See *Southern Life in Southern Literature,* Fulton, p. 259, 502. Whorten, p. 47.

[30] See note 8 ante.

[31] A war poem which moistens the eyes is Emily J. Moore's *Tell the Boys the War Is Ended.* It recalls an incident when the poet was visiting an army hospital in Rome, Georgia. There she saw a young soldier from an Arkansas regiment. He had been seriously wounded in the charge at Murfreesboro. He called her to his bedside and she saw at once that the gallant lad was dying. As she bent over him the young soldier was just able to whisper: "Tell the boys the War is ended."

[32] The text of this poem is found in *Southern Selections from the Southern Poets* (Weber) 1923 at p. 158. A sketch of the poem is found in *Southern Life in Southern Literature,* Fulton, (1917) at p. 296 and the poem appears there at p. 298. For a brief biographical sketch, see p. 391, *Southern Poets* (Parks), 1936.

[33] No biographical data could be found.

[34] This poem is thought to have been written at Camp Chase, Maryland, in December, 1861. The poem and a valuable note will be found at pp. 96-97 *Cullings from the Confederacy.* A memorial poem to Colonel Hawkins will be found at p. 544 of Miss Sally A. Brock's *The Southern Amaranth* (New York, 1869).

[35] Father Abram Joseph Ryan, the Poet-Priest of the Confederacy was intensely loyal to the new nation in its quest for independence. He lost his brother in battle for the Great Cause and he, himself, was a chaplain. He wrote the poem "C.S.A." to immortalize the members of the Confederate armed forces who gave their lives in battle. The second stanza was inscribed on the Tomb of the Unknown Soldier of the Confederate States of America at the Beauvoir Cemetery at Beauvoir, The Jefferson Davis Shrine, Biloxi, Mississippi.

AUTHOR INDEX